Original title:
Starlight Sleepover

Copyright © 2024 Creative Arts Management OÜ
All rights reserved.

Author: Evelyn Hartman
ISBN HARDBACK: 978-9916-90-532-6
ISBN PAPERBACK: 978-9916-90-533-3

Aurora Horizons

Dancing lights in the sky,
Awakening the night,
Colors swirl and combine,
Nature's pure delight.

Whispers of the dawn breeze,
Softly caressing trees,
A canvas painted bright,
In a dreamlike flight.

As the stars fade away,
Morning takes its claim,
Golden rays emerge,
Lighting up the same.

In this fleeting moment,
We find our peace again,
Wrapped in hues of glory,
A tranquil refrain.

Celestial Chill

Moonlight drapes the earth,
A silvery embrace,
Stars twinkle in delight,
In the vastness of space.

Frosty air whispers low,
Secrets of the night,
Crystals on the leaves glow,
Sparkling with pure light.

Underneath the cosmos,
Time seems to stand still,
In the stillness we find,
A warmth that can fulfill.

As shadows stretch and yawn,
Dreams beckon us near,
Wrapped in a celestial chill,
We shed every fear.

Illuminated Imaginings

In the depth of the mind,
Colors blend and spark,
Visions dance and twirl,
Igniting the dark.

Brush strokes of the heart,
Paint the silent air,
Dreams becoming real,
With love beyond compare.

Every thought a whisper,
Casting shadows wide,
Imaginations roam,
On a colorful tide.

With each fleeting moment,
We create our own light,
Illuminated imaginings,
Guide us through the night.

Cosmic Refuge

In the silence of space,
A refuge we find,
Stars sing a soft hymn,
Echoing through the mind.

Galaxies in motion,
Calm within the storm,
A shelter from the chaos,
In the universe's form.

Gravity pulls us closer,
To wonders untold,
In this cosmic embrace,
We let go of the cold.

Together we will soar,
Through the vast unknown,
In this cosmic refuge,
We have found our home.

Celestial Chit-Chat

Stars twinkle high above,
Soft whispers in the night.
Moonbeams dance on shadows,
Guiding dreams to take flight.

Galaxies spin and swirl,
In a cosmic embrace.
Comets race through the dark,
A stellar, silent chase.

Planets hum their own tunes,
A harmony so sweet.
Each note a gentle breeze,
Beneath our wandering feet.

In this vast, endless space,
Thoughts drift like clouds in air.
A universe of thoughts,
Shared in moments rare.

Nightfall Murmurs

The sun dips below the hills,
Whispers fill the evening.
Crickets play their serenade,
Nature's soft believing.

Shadows stretch and grow long,
Stars begin to peek through.
Nightfall wraps the world tight,
With a blanket of blue.

The moon shares secret tales,
With the rivers that flow.
Each ripple holds a story,
Of all the things we know.

Breezes carry sweet smells,
Of earth and dreams combined.
In this tranquil moment,
Peace is well-defined.

Twilight Tales

The sun fades golden hues,
Whispers of the day close.
Colors blend in harmony,
As evening gently grows.

Fireflies join the dance,
Glowing like tiny stars.
Their light a playful wink,
From dusk to night, so far.

Tales from ancient shadows,
Echo through the trees.
Each rustle, every sound,
Carried on the breeze.

In twilight's gentle arms,
The universe sighs low.
Magic fills the twilight,
In the fading glow.

Cosmic Dreamscapes

In dreams, we soar like birds,
Through galaxies unseen.
Nebulae call our names,
In colors rich and keen.

Black holes whisper secrets,
Of time that bends and sways.
Floating on cosmic seas,
In an astral haze.

Wonders paint the night sky,
In strokes of starlight bright.
Each vision, a journey,
In the depths of the night.

With the moon as our guide,
We wander far and wide.
In these cosmic dreamscapes,
Our imaginations glide.

Moonlit Musings

Under the silver glow,
Whispers of the night,
Dreams begin to flow,
In soft, gentle light.

Silhouettes of trees,
Swaying in the breeze,
Secrets shared with stars,
Echoing from afar.

Rippling waters sigh,
Reflecting the moon,
As time drifts by,
In a quiet tune.

Lost in thought's embrace,
Where shadows dance slow,
In this sacred space,
The heart starts to glow.

Ethereal Encounters

In a realm so bright,
Where the day meets the night,
Figures of pure grace,
In an endless chase.

Voices softly call,
In a dreamlike thrall,
Glimmers in the air,
Floating everywhere.

Moments weave and twine,
Like threads of the divine,
Turning time to dust,
In hope we all trust.

Lost between the lines,
Where the spirit shines,
All that one might seek,
In silence, we speak.

Frosted Galaxy

Stars adorned in white,
Twinkling in the cold,
Frozen in the night,
Stories yet untold.

Nebulas bloom bright,
In a cosmic dance,
Shining with delight,
A timeless romance.

Planets spin in grace,
In their steady race,
Crystals of the night,
Glinting in their flight.

Wonders far and near,
In the silent sphere,
Underneath the hue,
I dream of the new.

Veil of Stars

In the velvet dark,
Glistening so high,
Each a secret spark,
Whispering goodbye.

Beneath the soft glow,
Wonders begin to show,
A tapestry spun,
By the glowing sun.

Celestial dreams soar,
Beyond the known shores,
In the night's embrace,
We find our own place.

Lost in the vast sea,
Where hearts wander free,
In this quiet night,
We embrace the light.

Beyond the Horizon

Waves crash gently on the shore,
Whispers of dreams forevermore.
Sunset glows with colors bright,
Calling us towards the night.

Footprints lead to the unknown,
Each step taken, seeds are sown.
Stars above begin to rise,
Winking softly from the skies.

In the distance, mountains call,
Veiled in shadows, proud and tall.
Adventure waits, so full of grace,
Beyond the horizon, dreams embrace.

Midnight Explorations

In the stillness of the night,
Softly gleams the silver light.
Whispers of the world awake,
Gentle paths that we will take.

Stars like lanterns in the dark,
Guide our journey, leave a mark.
Footprints traced on hidden trails,
In the silence, wonder sails.

Echoes of the night's sweet song,
Call us forth, where we belong.
Midnight secrets, dreams untold,
In our hearts, a fire bold.

Celestial Connections

In twilight's embrace, we find our way,
Stars align to light our play.
Galaxies whispering ancient lore,
Shared by spirits, forevermore.

Comets streak through velvet skies,
Drawing hopes like hidden ties.
In the cosmos, love intertwines,
As soulmates dance, through vast designs.

Connections forged through endless space,
Time and matter, we embrace.
Eternal bonds that never sever,
In this universe, we are forever.

Velvet Skies

Underneath the velvet skies,
Dreamers gaze with hopeful eyes.
Moonlight glimmers on the sea,
Whispering tales of you and me.

Night unfolds like softest dreams,
Wrapped in warmth, a world that gleams.
Stars like diamonds, brightly shine,
In this moment, hearts align.

Breezes dance with sweet delight,
Carrying wishes to the night.
In the stillness, love ignites,
Painting shadows with our lights.

Dreamy Journey Under Stars

Beneath the velvet night,
Our dreams take flight.
The stars a guiding map,
In twilight's gentle lap.

Through constellations bright,
We sail on silver light.
Whispers of hope unfold,
In stories yet untold.

With moonbeams as our sail,
We drift on a soft gale.
Each twinkle sparks delight,
In this serene night.

As dawn begins to break,
Our hearts will softly ache.
For in this dreamy sphere,
Magic lingers near.

Whispered Wishes

In the still of the night,
Wishes take their flight.
Whispers weave through air,
Secrets everywhere.

Stars blink above us now,
With a solemn vow.
Carrying dreams on high,
Like birds in the sky.

With every heartfelt plea,
They dance wild and free.
Carved from hopes and dreams,
Flowing like silver streams.

Beneath the moon's soft gaze,
In a dreamy haze.
We cherish every thread,
Of the wishes we've said.

Under the Whispering Skies

Under skies so wide,
We wander side by side.
With every breath we take,
New memories we make.

The winds sing a tune,
Guiding us toward the moon.
Stars sprinkle down their light,
Filling our hearts with delight.

In the hush of the night,
Everything feels right.
Nature's gentle sighs,
Beneath whispering skies.

As dreams intertwine,
In the glow so divine.
We travel hand in hand,
Across this magic land.

Celestial Cabins

In cosmic cabins bright,
Where stars ignite the night.
Floating on stardust's grace,
In this enchanted space.

Each cabin holds a dream,
Beyond what we can deem.
A sanctuary fair,
With wishes in the air.

Galaxies softly hum,
In a rhythm, we become.
With every wish we share,
The universe laid bare.

So let our spirits soar,
To realms we've not explored.
In celestial embrace,
We find our sacred place.

Aurora's Gentle Caress

In whispers soft, the dawn is near,
The sky adorns its colors clear.
A dance of light, a tender hue,
Embracing all, the world anew.

With each ray's touch, the shadows flee,
Awakening life, a symphony.
The flowers stretch, the birds take flight,
In Aurora's arms, the day feels right.

Flickers of Fantasy

In twilight's glow, dreams take their form,
Realms of wonder, a magic storm.
Whispers of tales from ages past,
In flickers bright, enchantments cast.

Beneath the stars, our hopes ignite,
In shadows deep, we chase the light.
With each heartbeat, a story spins,
In fantasies where adventure begins.

Celestial Campfire Chat

Beneath the stars, we gather round,
With shared stories, our hearts abound.
The fire crackles, the night is still,
In laughter's glow, time seems to thrill.

With every flicker, secrets flow,
Of cosmic dreams and worlds we know.
A bond that glows, like embers bright,
In this celestial, wondrous night.

Echoes of Enchanted Slumber

In gentle hush, the dreamers sigh,
As starlit visions drift on by.
Lost in realms where magic reigns,
In slumber's grip, our spirit gains.

With every breath, a tale unfolds,
Of whispered myths and love retold.
As echoes fade, the night holds tight,
In enchanted realms, we find our light.

Cosmic Restlessness

Stars whisper secrets through the night,
Galaxies spin in a shimmering flight.
A comet streaks with a fleeting grace,
Restless souls wander through infinite space.

Planets collide in a cosmic dance,
Chasing the shadows, lost in a trance.
Time bends where the wonders reside,
In the vastness, our dreams collide.

Nocturnal Nuances

Silvery moonlight kisses the ground,
Night's gentle whispers are all around.
Crickets croon in the cool evening air,
Dreams drift softly, without a care.

The velvet sky holds a thousand lights,
Filling the darkness with shimmering sights.
Each star a story, a wish to bestow,
In the still of night, our hearts overflow.

Midnight Meditations

In the calm of midnight, thoughts arise,
Silent reflections under the skies.
Whispers of wisdom echo within,
A journey begins as the stillness spins.

Breath in the shadows, release all fears,
Embrace the stillness, the wisdom appears.
Moments of peace in the depth of night,
Lighting the path with soft, golden light.

Falling into Dreams

Drift on a cloud, let the worries flee,
Fall into dreams, wild and free.
The world fades softly into the mist,
Cradled in starlight, you can't resist.

Colors swirl in a fantastical scheme,
Eyes gently close, surrender to dream.
Awake in the morning, with visions anew,
Each night a canvas, each dream a hue.

Dreamcatcher's Embrace

In the night sky, soft whispers flow,
Hopes and memories drifting low.
Threads of dreams in silence weave,
Captured moments, we believe.

Stars like beads on a gentle strand,
Grasping joy with a tender hand.
Resting hearts in peace they find,
Dreams entwined, forever kind.

Beneath the moon's watchful face,
Fears and worries find their place.
With each dawn, new paths arise,
Guided gently by the skies.

In the stillness, life exhales,
Through the night, love never fails.
With a touch, our spirits soar,
In dreamcatcher's embrace, we explore.

Constellation Stories

Once upon a twinkling night,
Stars unfolded tales of light.
Every spark, a memory shared,
Whispers carried, souls ensnared.

A warrior's heart, a lover's plea,
Maps of dreams for all to see.
In the vastness, legends spun,
Echoes of what's lost and won.

Galaxies weave a timeless lore,
Of distant lands and open doors.
Charting paths through endless skies,
Constellations that never die.

In the darkness, stories glow,
Lighting hearts with every throw.
Each constellation, a guide true,
Carving hope in shades of blue.

Nocturnal Soiree

Beneath the stars, shadows dance,
In the stillness, a whispered chance.
Laughter echoes through the air,
In twilight's grace, we lose our care.

Moonlit paths invite us near,
With every step, the night is clear.
A symphony of crickets play,
As dreams awaken, come what may.

Sharing stories, secrets spilled,
In every heart, the night is filled.
With starlight shines in twinkling hues,
Our souls entwined in midnight's muse.

Embers glow in the fleeting night,
We cherish moments, hold them tight.
Nocturnal soiree, spirits free,
Together in this reverie.

Celestial Wonderment

In the cosmos, wonders bloom,
Galaxies swirl in endless loom.
Stardust kisses all we see,
A canvas bright, our mystery.

Nebulae in colors bright,
Painting dreams in silent flight.
Whispers of the universe call,
Reminders of how small we fall.

Planets turn with graceful ease,
Bathed in hues of cosmic tease.
Infinite space, a boundless sea,
A celestial dance, wild and free.

In the night, our spirits chase,
Each sparkling point, a warm embrace.
Celestial wonderment unfolds,
The universe, a tale retold.

The Quiet of the Cosmos

In the stillness of the night,
Stars whisper secrets, shining bright.
Galaxies swirl in silent dance,
While dreams unfold, given a chance.

The moon hangs low, a silver sigh,
Casting shadows, as time slips by.
Planets spin in their gentle grace,
Echoes of existence in endless space.

Each twinkle tells a tale untold,
Of ancient wanderers, brave and bold.
The universe breathes a calming tune,
A lullaby beneath the glowing moon.

Lost in thought, we gaze in awe,
At the vastness, we just withdraw.
In the quiet of the cosmos wide,
We find our heartbeats, calm and tied.

Lullabies Under a Painted Sky

At dusk the world begins to fade,
Colors dance, their beauty laid.
Crimson clouds and golden rays,
Whisper songs of ending days.

The horizon wraps in soft embrace,
As fireflies light their timeless race.
Gentle breezes hum a tune,
Lulling dreams beneath the moon.

Stars peek out, a shimmering host,
Guiding wishes, our hearts engrossed.
Each twinkling light, a gentle sigh,
Lovestruck moments as time drifts by.

Underneath this painted sky,
Softly we breathe, and softly sigh.
Wrapped in wonders, our spirits soar,
Lullabies echo, forevermore.

Stars as Our Witness

In the velvet night, we stand aglow,
Beneath the stars' eternal show.
They witness dreams spun from our hearts,
As wishes take flight, like shooting sparks.

In whispered secrets, shadows twine,
Love's sweet laughter, delicate line.
Galaxies twinkle, our hopes ignite,
Stars as our witness in the quiet night.

A tapestry of glimmering light,
Each pinprick promises, shining bright.
In cosmic silence, we share our fate,
Hearts aligned, through time we await.

Together we dance, shadows entwined,
With each soft glow, our souls aligned.
Stars watch over, our dreams released,
In the vast expanse, heartbeats increased.

Midnight Marshmallows and Memories

By the fire, embers glow red,
Whispers of stories, softly said.
Marshmallows toast on sticks held high,
Melting moments as the stars sigh.

In laughter shared, the night unfolds,
Each memory crafted, precious gold.
Sweet taste lingers, warm and light,
Underneath the blanket of the night.

Fireflies dance, a flickering show,
As we recall the tales we know.
Friendship's flames, they brightly burn,
In these moments, we forever yearn.

Midnight magic wraps us tight,
With every spark, we feel the light.
Marshmallows melt, memories stay,
In heart's embrace, come what may.

Astral Adventures

Through realms of stars we soar and glide,
On cosmic winds, we take our ride.
With comets bright, we dance and play,
In endless night, we find our way.

Across the void, our spirits dart,
A galaxy, a work of art.
With planets near and moons so far,
We chase our dreams, our dreams are stars.

Twinkling Twilight Talks

Beneath the sky, where shadows blend,
In whispered tones, our hearts suspend.
Each twinkle holds a secret bright,
In twilight's grasp, we share the light.

Stories told in starlit eyes,
Dreams unfolding like the skies.
With every word, the night grows deep,
In twilight talks, our souls we keep.

Moonbeam Magic

In silver light, the world does glow,
Casting dreams in softest flow.
With whispers hushed, we weave our charms,
In moonbeam magic, we find our arms.

Dancing shadows, a gentle sway,
Under the moon, we drift away.
In every glow, a promise made,
In moonlight soft, our fears will fade.

Galactic Gatherings

Stars aligned in cosmic dance,
Where spirits meet, and dreams enhance.
A tapestry of colors bright,
In galactic gatherings, we feel the light.

Voices blend in harmony,
Across the vast, in unity.
With hearts entwined and laughter shared,
In galaxies wide, our dreams declared.

Starlit Chronicles

In the night sky, tales unfold,
Whispers of dreams, shimmering bold.
Constellations dance, a cosmic show,
Guiding our hearts where hopes can flow.

Secrets of old in stardust sown,
Infinite paths, the night has grown.
With each twinkle, a story told,
A universe vast, where wonders unfold.

Soft light spills on the sleeping earth,
Kindling the spark of magic's birth.
Each star a wish, a voice in the dark,
Illuminating souls, igniting the spark.

Together we stand, beneath this dome,
Lost in the weave of the skies we call home.
In starlit chronicles, we'll find our way,
Mapping the night till the break of day.

Sighs Among the Stars

The moon hangs low, a gentle sigh,
Stars twinkle softly, drifting by.
Silent wishes float in the air,
Echoes of dreams laid bare with care.

Each glimmering light, a story there,
Moments captured in the midnight stare.
Whispers of love in the cool night breeze,
Swirling together, hearts find ease.

In cosmic ballet, we sway and spin,
Holding our breath as the night draws in.
With every breath, we softly share,
Sighs among the stars, a secret pair.

Wrapped in shadows, the world fades fast,
Guided by starlight, our hearts steadfast.
In this moment, the universe glows,
As deep connections blossom and pose.

The Weight of Wishes

Beneath the veil of twilight's grace,
We toss our dreams into open space.
Each wish a feather, light as air,
Hovering softly, a hope laid bare.

With every heartbeat, a longing grows,
The weight of wishes, like drifting throes.
In the silence, prayers softly hum,
Waiting to hear what the night will drum.

A tapestry woven of hopes and fears,
Threads of starlight, kissed by tears.
In the shadows, we quietly plead,
For the universe to plant the seed.

As dawn approaches, dreams take flight,
The weight of wishes ignites the night.
A chorus of hearts, entwined in trust,
Whispers of fate, in stardust we must.

Astral Adrift

Sailing the cosmos on whispers of night,
Floating through galaxies, lost in delight.
Stars beckon gently, inviting the dream,
In this vast expanse, nothing's as it seems.

Caught in the currents of cosmic streams,
Carried away on celestial beams.
A dance with the planets, a glide with the sun,
Astral adrift, where time comes undone.

Nebulas swirl in colors so bright,
Guiding the wanderer's heart in flight.
Each moment a treasure, both fleeting and rare,
In the cradle of stardust, we breathe the air.

Together we drift through the endless sea,
Exploring the wonders of what might be.
In this astral realm, so wild and free,
We find our place in eternity.

Mythical Moonlight

Veils of silver light do grace,
The gentle night, a soft embrace.
Whispers call from shadowed trees,
As magic dances on the breeze.

Glimmers flash in starry seas,
Echoes carried by the leaves.
Each beam holds a hidden tale,
In moonlit dreams, we will not pale.

The world transforms in night's caress,
With secrets wrapped in emptiness.
From heights above, we are watched near,
In mythical realms, void of fear.

So let us roam 'neath glowing skies,
Where hopes take flight, and spirit flies.
In moonlit paths, our hearts align,
Within the night, the stars entwine.

Whispers of the Cosmos

In quiet realms where stardust swirls,
The cosmos hums, its beauty unfurls.
Galaxies spin, in harmony bright,
Whispers echo through the endless night.

Each star a dream, each planet a song,
In celestial dance, we all belong.
Time bends softly, lost in its glow,
As secrets hidden begin to flow.

Celestial winds carry our sighs,
And wrap us tight 'neath haunting skies.
We're woven threads in time's vast loom,
In cosmic tales, we find our bloom.

So gaze above, let your spirit soar,
Embrace the whispers forever more.
Within the vast, where wonders gleam,
We are but echoes of a dream.

Starstruck Gatherings

Underneath the night so clear,
We gather 'round, there's naught to fear.
In laughter's glow, connections spark,
A constellation ignites the dark.

Stories shared in twinkling light,
Friendships woven, hearts take flight.
Above us glimmer, tales untold,
In starstruck gatherings, brave and bold.

With each shared glance, the world unites,
Moments captured in starry sights.
Beneath the vast, our spirits sing,
In every heartbeat, joy we bring.

So let us dance, and let us play,
In the magic of this starry array.
Together we shine, both near and far,
In gatherings bright, we are each a star.

Infinite Dreams

In realms where visions intertwine,
Infinite dreams on pathways shine.
A tapestry of hopes unfurled,
Where every thought can change the world.

In quiet whispers, secrets breathe,
In every heart, the will to weave.
Imagination bursts like flames,
In silent nights, we chase our aims.

Through vibrant colors, truth will flow,
Beyond the stars, the spirit knows.
Each dream a key, each wish a door,
To worlds unknown, forevermore.

So close your eyes, let wonders beam,
In slumber's grasp, embrace the dream.
For in those depths, we find our way,
To endless nights and brighter days.

Celestial Comforts

Underneath the twinkling skies,
Whispers of the night arise,
Moonlight bathes the earth in peace,
Softly, all our worries cease.

Stars like diamonds scattered wide,
Guide our thoughts to dreams inside,
With each breath, we feel embraced,
In this calm, our hearts are graced.

Nature sings a lullaby,
As the world begins to sigh,
Wrapped in warmth of night's caress,
Here we find our happiness.

In celestial realms we dwell,
Stories only stars can tell,
Floating on this tranquil sea,
Forever, you and I are free.

Starlit Reverie

Glistening gems adorn the night,
Dreamers dance in silver light,
Thoughts like fireflies softly glow,
In this magic, love will flow.

Nebulas weave a tapestry,
Filling hearts with mystery,
Each wish cast upon the breeze,
Stirs the cosmos with such ease.

Time is lost in endless space,
Every glance a warm embrace,
In this realm where shadows play,
Starlit dreams will lead the way.

With the dawn, the dream will fade,
Yet the echoes will not jade,
In our hearts, the spark remains,
Memories that love sustains.

Ethereal Night Revelry

A canopy of velvet skies,
Where the moonlight softly lies,
Every star, a fleeting wish,
In the night, our spirits swish.

Joyful laughter fills the air,
Echoes dancing everywhere,
In a waltz of gentle dreams,
Life, more vibrant than it seems.

With the night as our parade,
Through the shadows love cascades,
Glowing hearts in unity,
Celebrate this mystery.

As dawn whispers its sweet refrain,
In our hearts, the joys remain,
Ethereal nights will inspire,
Kindling our eternal fire.

Cosmic Cauldron of Dreams

In the quiet of the night,
Cosmic wonders take their flight,
In the cauldron, dreams are brewed,
Stirrings of the heart renewed.

Galaxies spin tales of old,
Of adventures yet untold,
Each moment a starry glance,
In this vast celestial dance.

Fires of passion softly glow,
In the night, our spirits flow,
Dreams unfurl like petals sweet,
Cosmic love in rhythmic beat.

With the dawn, our dreams may fade,
Yet the night, it will cascade,
In the cosmos, we will find,
Echoes of love intertwined.

Whispering Silhouettes

In the dusk, shadows play,
Whispers of the fading day.
Silhouettes dance in the light,
A gentle touch, a soft flight.

Underneath the silver moon,
Echoes hum a sweet tune.
Dreams take shape in dimmed glow,
Carried by the evening's flow.

Every sigh, a secret shared,
In the dark, hearts laid bare.
Softened breaths, a hushed embrace,
Time stills in this sacred space.

With each moment, shadows blend,
Whispering tales that never end.
In the night, forever friends,
Silhouettes where magic bends.

Nebula Nights

Stars ignite the velvet skies,
A canvas where the cosmos lies.
Nebulas swirl with colors bright,
Painting dreams in the still of night.

Galaxies spin in distant light,
Whispers of stories taking flight.
Celestial wonders, a vast expanse,
Invite our hearts to dream and dance.

In the depths of this galaxy wide,
Our hopes and dreams we will confide.
Each twinkle holds a wish unspun,
In nebula nights, we are as one.

Beneath the stars, we find our way,
In cosmic realms, we long to stay.
Lost in wonder, forever in sight,
Embraced by the beauty of nebula night.

Starlit Storytelling

Beneath the stars, tales unfold,
Whispers of life, both daring and bold.
Each shimmer a story, old yet new,
Revealing secrets of me and you.

Candles flicker, shadows bloom,
In the night, dispelling gloom.
Words woven softly, like a spell,
Starlit air carries them well.

Silent laughter fills the space,
Every glance a warm embrace.
In this hush, time gently slows,
With every heartbeat, the magic grows.

As dawn approaches, stories remain,
In starlit whispers, they sustain.
A tapestry of dreams retold,
Forever cherished, forever bold.

Dreamy Embraces

In twilight's grasp, soft and sweet,
Dreamy visions, a joyful beat.
Tender moments, softly shared,
In embraces, hearts laid bare.

Lulled by stars in velvet skies,
We chase the whispers, hear their cries.
Wrapped in warmth, lost in bliss,
Every heartbeat seals a kiss.

Gentle sighs weave a thread,
In the realm where dreams are fed.
Floating softly, like a breeze,
In this space, our spirits tease.

As night unfolds, we drift away,
In dreamy embraces, we wish to stay.
Carved in twilight, forever traced,
In the magic of love's embrace.

Magical Midnight Moments

Moonlight dances on the stream,
Whispers weave a silent dream.
Stars above begin to glow,
As the night begins to flow.

Softly sighing, breezes hum,
In the dark, the shadows drum.
Each heartbeat ties the night so tight,
Creating magic in the light.

Glimmers spark in distant skies,
Wonder glows in sleepy eyes.
Every second feels like gold,
In these moments, dreams unfold.

Time stands still, a breath so slight,
As we wander through the night.
Every glance, a story told,
In the midnight's magic, bold.

Luminous Lullabies

Crickets sing a gentle tune,
Underneath the silver moon.
Dreams take flight on whispered wings,
In the night, serenity sings.

Softest shadows start to play,
Guiding us till break of day.
Every star a lullaby,
In the dark, where hearts can fly.

Close your eyes and breathe it in,
Feel the world begin to spin.
Wrapped in warmth, the night will keep,
As you sink in tranquil sleep.

Let the night embrace you tight,
Filling dreams with soft moonlight.
In the hush, the magic lies,
Drifting off to lullabies.

Enigmatic Nights

Mystery cloaks the night so deep,
Secrets hide where shadows creep.
Whispers echo, soft and low,
As the twilight begins to flow.

Lost in thoughts, we wander far,
Guided by the evening star.
Every breath a silent plea,
In the stillness, just to be.

Twinkling lights in velvet skies,
Hold the wonders of our sighs.
Each moment wrapped in quiet grace,
As we seek a warm embrace.

Veils of night create the lure,
In its depth, we find the pure.
Every glance a fleeting chance,
To unravel night's romance.

Cosmic Conversations

Underneath a blanket wide,
Where the universe confides.
Sparkling dust of dreams and light,
Ignites thoughts in the still night.

Galaxies spin with tales untold,
In the dark, our hearts unfold.
Stardust dances on the breeze,
As we share our mysteries.

Waves of light that kiss the soul,
Whispering secrets, making whole.
Every heartbeat, a new quest,
In the cosmos, we find rest.

Stars above our silent friends,
Guiding us, where the night begins.
In their glow, our spirits rise,
Through cosmic talks, we touch the skies.

Dreamscapes of Dusk

Whispers dance on twilight beams,
As shadows twine in secret dreams.
The sky wears hues of soft embrace,
Where silence drapes a gentle face.

Lights flicker in the fading glow,
While stars awaken, soft and slow.
Night wraps the world in velvet care,
In dreams we wander, unaware.

With every sigh of evening deep,
The heart unfurls and starts to leap.
In dusk's domain, the soul finds rest,
A tranquil place, a sacred nest.

As colors fade and shadows blend,
We drift towards a whispered end.
In dreamscapes where the heart takes flight,
We chase the wonders of the night.

Moonlight Mischief

Beneath the silver moonlit gaze,
The world transforms in wild ways.
With laughter soft and secrets shared,
The night unfolds, gently bared.

A playful breeze stirs phantom leaves,
As nature weaves its midnight thieves.
Stars twinkle with a knowing wink,
Inviting hearts to pause and think.

The shadows stretch, the echoes hum,
While mischief brews, a gentle drum.
In lunar light, the jesters play,
To steal the calm of night away.

With every jest, the dreams arise,
In moonlit realms, we lose our ties.
In mischief wrapped, a fleeting bliss,
We find the magic in a kiss.

Fantastical Nightscape

In night's embrace, the wonders bloom,
A tapestry of silk and gloom.
Each star a tale, each shadow cast,
A fantastical realm unsurpassed.

The moon, a lantern hung on high,
Illuminates the velvet sky.
Creatures roam in whispered grace,
In dreams, we drift from place to place.

A river flows with silver beams,
Reflecting all our wildest dreams.
Mountains rise with jagged peaks,
Where magic sings and silence speaks.

In every corner, stories hide,
In fantastical worlds, dreams abide.
The night unveils its endless lore,
Inviting us to seek and soar.

Celestial Haven

Upon the canvas, stars are sown,
In celestial haven, hearts have grown.
With every twinkle, hope ignites,
A refuge found in endless nights.

The universe spins a tale so wide,
With cosmic wonders as our guide.
In every heartbeat, galaxies sway,
A dance of light that leads the way.

Through nebulae with hues ablaze,
We wander lost in astral maze.
Embraced by grace of infinite skies,
We find our peace as the stardust flies.

In this divine, eternal space,
We linger on, both slow and haste.
In celestial haven, dreams take flight,
We drift forever in the night.

Glittering Sky Retreat

Under the stars, we lay so still,
Whispers of dreams beneath the chill.
A canvas of night, so vast and grand,
Holding our secrets, hand in hand.

Crickets sing soft in twilight's breath,
Nature's lullaby, a gentle caress.
Fireflies flicker, a dance of light,
Guiding our hearts through the cool night.

The world fades away, it's just we two,
In this retreat, where love feels new.
Moonbeams kiss the earth's gentle edge,
Promising moments, a lover's pledge.

As comets streak through the velvet dome,
Together we weave our dreams, our home.
In the glittering sky, we find our place,
Forever lost in this starlit space.

Moonlight Gatherings

Gathered beneath the silver glow,
Laughter lingers, soft and low.
Friends entwined in stories shared,
In moonlight's magic, we are bared.

The night wraps us in a tender embrace,
Every word spoken, a warm trace.
Stars twinkle softly, a mindful cheer,
Unity thrives, as hearts draw near.

Time suspends in this sacred hour,
Bonds grow stronger, like blooming flowers.
With every tale, the shadows sway,
Creating memories that will never fray.

So let the moon bear witness tonight,
To our gathering, pure delight.
In this luminous world, we are free,
Together forever, just you and me.

Twinkling Fantasies

In the hush of night, where wishes gleam,
Twinkling fantasies weave through the dream.
Sparkles of hope dance in the air,
Guiding our hearts, a love so rare.

We chase the stars with eyes wide bright,
Lost in the whispers of silvery light.
Every eyelash wish, a flickering flame,
Unraveling stories, never the same.

Echoes of laughter fill the whole space,
Twinkling visions, a velvet embrace.
In this realm where magic prevails,
We soar above on ethereal trails.

The night paints dreams with colors bold,
Of memories cherished, stories told.
In twinkling fantasies, let us reside,
Together forever, side by side.

Midnight Caravan

A caravan rolls under the crescent moon,
Whispers of secrets, a theatrical tune.
With every mile, we leave behind,
The world of worries, the ties that bind.

Fires flicker with tales of the night,
Casting shadows, a beautiful sight.
The desert winds carry our laughter high,
As stars become lanterns, lighting the sky.

Each stop reveals wonders untold,
With stories of love, courage, and gold.
In the heart of the night, we roam so free,
This midnight caravan, just you and me.

Time becomes endless, a pause so sweet,
Each moment we share, a treasured heartbeat.
With dreams as our guide through the darkened sea,
Together we'll wander, just you and me.

Starlit Escapades

In the quiet of the night,
Whispers of dreams take flight.
Beneath the moon's gentle gaze,
Wanderers find their hidden ways.

Through meadows soft and serene,
Stars paint the sky, a shimmering scene.
Adventures call, a siren's song,
Together in magic, where we belong.

Under the canopy of twinkling lights,
We chase the shadows, heartbeats ignite.
Hand in hand, we dare to roam,
In every heartbeat, we find our home.

With laughter echoing soft and clear,
We weave tales of joy, with nothing to fear.
As constellations guide our quest,
In starlit escapades, we find our rest.

Nighttime Narratives

In the hush of the evening's glow,
Stories arise, like rivers flow.
Moonlit paths tell tales untold,
Whispers of wisdom, soft and bold.

Chasing shadows, we seek delight,
In the depth of the starry night.
Every twinkle a word, every breeze a phrase,
Crafting our moments, a tapestry of days.

With the universe as our open book,
We dive into realms with a curious look.
The night unfolds, a canvas so wide,
In nighttime narratives, we take our ride.

Eager hearts and open minds,
Find magic in the moon's designs.
With every tale and every sigh,
We write our stories 'neath the sky.

Aurora Borealis Bliss

Dancing lights in the northern sky,
Whispers of wonder, they flutter by.
Colors collide in a vibrant embrace,
Nature's canvas, a celestial grace.

With every hue, the darkness fades,
As dreams awaken, gently cascades.
A tapestry woven of emerald and gold,
In aurora's arms, our spirits unfold.

We gaze in awe, enchanted by sight,
Chasing the glow, the magic of night.
Under this wonder, hearts ignite,
In the beauty of bliss, we find delight.

Voices hushed, as if time stands still,
Nature's symphony, we feel the thrill.
In every sparkle, a story awaits,
In aurora borealis, love celebrates.

Celestial Conferences

In gatherings beyond the stars,
We share our dreams; it's never far.
Galaxies whisper, planets align,
In celestial conferences, we intertwine.

Voices of comets, tales of the sun,
Gathering wisdom, we become one.
In this celestial dance, we find our place,
As constellations guide us in grace.

Time stands still in this cosmic space,
Where light years merge in a warm embrace.
With stardust knowledge, we explore,
Unlocking the mysteries forevermore.

Every moment sparkles, every thought shines,
In eternal circles, our fate aligns.
In harmony under the night's vast dome,
Celestial conferences lead us home.

Twilight Tales and Tucked-In Secrets

In twilight's hush, the stories weave,
Ghosts of dreams that we believe.
Whispers float on gentle dusk,
Tucked in tight, like precious husk.

Shadows dance on silver dew,
Memories whisper, soft and true.
Underneath the silver moon,
Hearts will hum a lullaby tune.

Stars awake with twinkling eyes,
Watching over our sweet sighs.
Every secret that we keep,
Softly blankets in our sleep.

Evening's cloak, a velvet deep,
Guarding all our dreams to seep.
With twilight tales and thoughts anew,
The night unfolds, a magic view.

Galaxy of Giggling Stars

In the night sky, laughter glows,
A galaxy where joy bestows.
Giggling stars in playful flight,
Painting dreams on canvas night.

With each tick of the cosmic clock,
Whispers of the universe rock.
Constellations twirl and spin,
Inviting us to join, dive in.

Wandering through the outer space,
Every twinkle, a smile on face.
Falling lights, like wishes stray,
Dancing softly, drifting away.

In this sky of endless schemes,
We drift on waves of stardust dreams.
Galaxy's giggles, pure and bright,
Guide us gently through the night.

Constellations and Candlelight

Beneath the stars, our stories spark,
Constellations glow, lighting the dark.
With candlelight, our shadows play,
We weave our hopes as night turns gray.

The Milky Way whispers soft and low,
As we share the secrets we know.
In flickering flame, our spirits dance,
Each fleeting moment, a sacred chance.

Guided by these twinkling jewels,
We gather dreams like precious tools.
The sky above, a canvas vast,
Holding echoes of our past.

In twilight's grace, our hearts ignite,
Fueling the flame, spirit's delight.
Constellations and candlelight shine,
Forever binding your heart with mine.

Slumbering Beneath the Milky Way

As the night wraps the world in peace,
Stars above bring silent release.
Slumbering dreams beneath the glow,
Of the Milky Way's gentle flow.

Each twinkling light, a lullaby,
Carried softly through the sky.
Floating on clouds, soft as air,
Whispers of love linger there.

In cosmic arms, we lose the hour,
Cradled gently by the starlight power.
With every sigh, the night unfolds,
A tapestry of dreams untold.

Beneath the vast and endless night,
We find our solace, pure delight.
Slumbering close, we drift away,
Together, 'neath the Milky Way.

Cosmic Companions

In the vastness of space, they wander free,
Stars twinkling gently, a cosmic spree.
Galaxies dancing in an endless waltz,
Together in silence, boundless, and vast.

Planets rotating, a celestial dance,
With moons that whisper, in night's advance.
Comets like dreams, with tails that gleam,
Cosmic companions in a starlit dream.

Nebulas blooming, colors ablaze,
Light-years away in a timeless haze.
Each twinkle a story from eons past,
In this universe, vast and unsurpassed.

Together we sigh, beneath the night sky,
Finding our place where the stars lie.
In cosmic embrace, we drift and explore,
For in this expanse, we are evermore.

Fables Under the Firmament

Tales of old echo in the night,
Whispers of wisdom, soft and light.
Beneath the moon's glow, stories unfold,
Fables of courage, of love, and of gold.

Stars become scribes, writing in time,
Every twinkle a verse, a rhythm, a rhyme.
Legends of heroes, of magic so bright,
Shared by the shadows that dance in the light.

The night holds a canvas, vast and deep,
Each constellation, a secret to keep.
In the stillness, we listen and learn,
For fables shared make the heart slowly yearn.

Under the firmament, dreams take their flight,
Carrying hope on the wings of the night.
In every tale told, a truth to find,
In the tapestry woven, the cosmos entwined.

Dreamcatchers in the Sky

In the hush of the night, dreams softly weave,
Threads of starlight, a gift to believe.
Caught in the silence, they twirl and sway,
Dreamcatchers hidden where the shadows play.

Whispers of wishes drift on the breeze,
Carried by moonbeams, among the trees.
Each fleeting thought, a delicate thread,
In the tapestry of night, where dreams are bred.

Softly they shimmer, like dew on the grass,
In the quiet moments, as moments pass.
Dreamcatchers whisper, while stars shine bright,
Guiding our dreams through the velvet night.

So let your heart wander, let your mind fly,
With the dreamcatchers woven in the sky.
For in every glimpse of the starlit array,
There lies a promise of a brand new day.

Whims of the Night

As dusk falls gently, secrets arise,
Whispers of magic under dark skies.
The night unfolds with a playful grin,
Inviting the wanderers, let the fun begin.

Moonbeams pirouette on the shimmering lake,
Each ripple a story that the water makes.
Shooting stars race through the velvet expanse,
In the whims of the night, we find our dance.

Shadows come alive with flickers of light,
Tales of adventure, of whimsy and flight.
In the heart of the night, we laugh and we twirl,
Lost in the magic, as dreams unfurl.

Under the blanket of glittering skies,
The world takes a breath, and the spirit flies.
Embrace the enchantment, let your soul ignite,
For life's sweetest moments are born of the night.

Velvet Nightfall

The moon whispers softly, high above,
While shadows dance gently, with dreams to weave.
Stars twinkle brightly, like diamonds in sky,
As night wraps the world, in velvet sighs.

Cool breezes linger, through trees they play,
Nature's sweet lullaby, at the end of day.
Crickets are singing, a chorus so wild,
Under the blanket, the world is a child.

Fireflies flicker, with magic they roam,
Each glow a reminder, that night feels like home.
The heart finds its peace, in the quiet embrace,
Of twilight's soft colors, a warm, gentle space.

In velvet nightfall, our worries take flight,
Wrapped in the stillness, till dawn greets the light.
With dreams intertwining, like threads made of gold,
We treasure the stories, each moment unfolds.

Comet's Caress

Across the vast heavens, a comet ignites,
Trails of bright stardust, in magical flights.
It whispers of wishes, in a shimmering glow,
A fleeting reminder, of dreams that we sow.

With each blazing sweep, it paints the dark skies,
A dance of enchantment, a spell that won't die.
Hold tight to your hopes, as it passes us by,
For in its embrace, all our dreams can fly.

A moment of wonder, where time seems to pause,
In the comet's caress, we find our true cause.
Let laughter and love be the echoes we hear,
With every bright journey, we conquer our fear.

As shadows draw close, and the night lingers on,
We'll chase after stardust, until the dawn.
In radiant glimmers, our spirits set free,
Comet's sweet caress is our destiny.

Shooting Star Secrets

When shooting stars streak, through the jevelled black,
They carry our secrets, as they race on track.
They dance on the edge, of the universe wide,
With each hopeful wish, our dreams they confide.

In hushed adoration, we gaze at the sky,
Waiting for sparks, to silently fly.
With each whispered promise, our hearts are alight,
As the night unfolds, in pure cosmic delight.

Time bends in the shimmer, of ether's soft light,
And all of our troubles fade into the night.
The mysteries deepen, in twinkling shows,
As secrets of starlight, around us bestow.

So let's dream together, beneath this vast dome,
With shooting stars guiding, we'll never feel alone.
Each flicker a tale, of what's yet to unfold,
In the universe's heart, our stories are told.

Dreamy Constellations

Up in the heavens, constellations align,
With stories of old, in a tapestry fine.
They whisper their myths, through the cool night air,
As we trace their journeys, with wonder and care.

In the dance of the heavens, we find our place,
A map of our dreams, in the cosmic embrace.
With every star's twinkle, a wish takes its flight,
In the world of the night, everything feels right.

Each pattern of light, holds a secret untold,
As our hearts beat with promises, new and bold.
Together we ponder, beneath endless skies,
Finding solace in shadows, where imagination lies.

So let's weave our dreams, with the stars shining bright,
In dreamy constellations, we celebrate night.
With the universe watching, we'll dance and we'll sing,
As moments together, become our own wing.

The Harmony of Hushed Laughter

In the garden where shadows play,
Soft giggles dance beneath the trees.
Echoes drift in the gentle sway,
As night weaves tales upon the breeze.

Moonlight paints the petals bright,
Whispers flutter in the air.
Stars awaken, a twinkling sight,
Laughter binds all without a care.

Every chuckle, a fleeting spark,
Beneath the sky, so vast and deep.
In the silence, we leave our mark,
Memories cherished, forever to keep.

Together, we find our soft refrain,
In the night, our spirits soar.
A harmony that can't explain,
Hushed laughter calls for evermore.

Under the Veil of Night

Stars hang low in the velvet sky,
Whispers flow like a gentle stream.
The moon, a pearl that draws the eye,
Cradles dreams within a dream.

Shadows dance where the cool winds sigh,
Secrets linger in twilight's embrace.
Beneath the stars, where wishes fly,
We lose ourselves in time and space.

Each hush of night, a promise made,
Soft caresses from the dark.
In silent worlds, our fears shall fade,
And illuminated paths embark.

Under the veil, hearts intertwine,
A place where all the lost can find.
Wrapped in night, your hand in mine,
Together, we leave the day behind.

Celestial Dreams

Drifting through a tapestry bright,
We chase the shadows of daylight.
In the cosmos, our hopes take flight,
Celestial whispers, pure delight.

Galaxies swirl in a cosmic dance,
Revealing paths of shimmering light.
Within the stars, we find our chance,
To roam the heavens, hearts in sight.

Each twinkle holds a story true,
Of futures waiting to unfold.
In the vast abyss, there's so much to do,
A universe rich with dreams untold.

Hold my hand, let's drift away,
To realms where wishes know no end.
In celestial dreams, together we stay,
As the night wraps us, our hearts transcend.

Nighttime Whispers

In the hush where shadows blend,
Softly spoken, the night descends.
A lullaby that knows no end,
Carried forth by gentle bends.

Crickets chirp a soothing tune,
Guiding secrets through the trees.
The world abandoned to the moon,
In whispered tones, we find our ease.

Every sigh, a tale to tell,
Woven deep in the fabric's thread.
In the stillness, all is well,
Our voices mingling, softly spread.

Nighttime whispers blend and sway,
A serenade of hearts that cling.
In this embrace, forever stay,
As dreams take flight on silken wing.

Luminous Slumber

In the quiet glow of night,
Stars whisper secrets, soft and bright.
Moonbeams dance on weary eyes,
Cradled dreams in velvet skies.

Gentle breezes gently sigh,
Carrying wishes, oh so high.
Wrapped in warmth, the world does fade,
In this bliss, our hearts cascade.

Clouds like pillows drift and sway,
In this realm, we softly play.
Luminous glimmers guide our way,
As night unfolds and shadows stay.

Slumber deep within its grace,
Find the peace in this safe space.
With every breath, let worries cease,
In luminous arms, we find our peace.

Enchanted Dreamsphere

Floating softly, stars take flight,
In the dreamsphere, pure delight.
Colors swirl like whispers rare,
Filling hearts with joy and care.

Gentle echoes of the night,
Calling forth our hearts' true light.
Magic weaves through every seam,
In this realm of whispered dream.

Creatures flit on silver beams,
Tales unfold in twilight streams.
In this world, time finds no end,
Every moment, curves and bends.

Awakening to morning's hue,
Memories bloom as skies turn blue.
The dreamsphere whispers soft and clear,
Holding magic, ever near.

Cosmic Campfire Tales

Beneath the stars, we gather round,
Campfire crackles, stories abound.
Fires dance with shadows long,
Echoes of a timeless song.

Tales of heroes, brave and bold,
Adventures spinning, dreams untold.
In the night, we find our place,
Unity in warmth, a golden space.

Galaxies twinkle, mysteries gleam,
In the firelight, we weave a dream.
Each narrative stirs the heart,
Intertwining, never apart.

As embers fade, let silence reign,
In cosmic realms, we feel no pain.
With every story, we ignite,
The heavens whisper through the night.

Aurora Lullabies

Dancing lights on velvet skies,
Auroras sing their soft lullabies.
Whispers wrapped in emerald glow,
Cradle dreams where gentle winds blow.

Each flutter paints the night anew,
Colors merging, vivid and true.
Nature's canvas, art divine,
In this moment, hearts entwine.

Sleep beneath the cosmic veil,
Where every star tells wondrous tales.
In the hush, let worries cease,
In aurora's arms, we find our peace.

As dawn approaches, colors blend,
Whispers of night, soft messages send.
Lullabies linger in the air,
Breath of magic everywhere.

The Nocturnal Embrace

In shadows deep, the moon does glow,
Whispers of night begin to flow.
The stars are stitched in velvet skies,
A hush unfolds as daylight dies.

Beneath the cloak of twilight's grace,
Hearts collide in a secret place.
The world outside begins to fade,
In dreams we're dancing, unafraid.

Soft breezes carry tales of old,
While mysteries in silence unfold.
Time stands still, a fleeting dance,
In this nocturnal, sweet romance.

So let us linger, just a while,
Embrace the night, its whispered smile.
In every shadow, love ignites,
Together lost in starry nights.

Dreams in the Dark

In silence deep, the dreams take flight,
Hidden wishes kiss the night.
Softly wrapped in velvet gloom,
Hope awakens in the room.

Stars begin their twinkling play,
Guiding spirits on their way.
Each thought a spark in shadowed space,
Embracing magic's sweet embrace.

Through whispers soft, the visions dance,
In every heartbeat lies a chance.
For in the dark, we find our way,
To brighter worlds where we can stay.

So close your eyes and let them lead,
The dreams you nurture, plant the seed.
In darkness, find the light that glows,
A tapestry of night that grows.

Shooting Stars and Sleepless Nights

Beneath the sky, where wishes flow,
Shooting stars in cosmic glow.
Time drips slowly, moments gleam,
In sleepless nights, we chase a dream.

The world is hushed, the heart awakes,
In twilight's arms, the silence breaks.
Dreams collide with hopes anew,
As starlit paths come into view.

A whispered wish, a longing sigh,
As constellations paint the sky.
In every heartbeat, life ignites,
Through shooting stars and endless nights.

Hold tight your dreams, let them unfold,
In nighttime's magic, brave and bold.
For every star that streaks above,
Carries with it, a tale of love.

A Blanket of Wishes

Wrapped in night, a blanket wide,
Covering dreams where hopes reside.
Each star a thought, a fleeting glance,
A universe that stirs and prance.

As shadows loom and silence reigns,
We gather wishes, freeing chains.
Through layers soft, we weave our hopes,
In whispered prayers, our spirit copes.

The fabric of the night enfolds,
Stories shared, and dreams retold.
In this cocoon, we dare to soar,
As wishes dance forevermore.

So close your eyes, let visions play,
Underneath the moonlit sway.
With every heartbeat, drift away,
A blanket of wishes holds the day.

Whispers Under the Cosmos

Beneath the stars, soft secrets flow,
Gentle winds carry tales of glow.
The night is draped in velvet black,
As dreams take flight on a silken track.

Shadows dance in the pale moonlight,
Bringing whispers that feel so right.
Every star a bright, twinkling eye,
Guarding wishes that drift and sigh.

Through the silence, hearts entwine,
In this wonder, we feel divine.
The universe hums a soothing song,
In the darkness, we both belong.

Lost in the magic, we gently sway,
Under the cosmos, come what may.
The night is ours, no fear of the dawn,
Together, we carry on, we carry on.

Celestial Dreams Unfold

In the twilight, dreams begin to soar,
Whispers of the cosmos call for more.
Stars twinkle like a thousand eyes,
Painting the canvas of midnight skies.

Each constellation tells a tale,
Of ancient love and ships that sail.
With every breath, we feel the weave,
Of cosmic threads that gently deceive.

Floating through realms of stardust bright,
We chase the echoes of the night.
Celestial wonders spin and twirl,
In this magical, dream-filled world.

Awake in dreams, we may transcend,
On this journey that has no end.
With hearts ignited by cosmic light,
In the sky, our spirits take flight.

Moonlit Gatherings

In the hush of night, under moon's embrace,
We gather close in this sacred space.
Laughter dances on whispers soft,
As time seems to linger and drift aloft.

Candles flicker in shadows cast,
Memories linger, the spell is vast.
Stories shared with a knowing glance,
In this stillness, hearts find their chance.

Glimmers of light upon our skin,
Breath in sync as we draw within.
Connected by dreams beneath the sky,
In moonlit gatherings, we freely fly.

Each moment precious, a treasure trove,
Embracing warmth, we gently strove.
Under the stars, together we thrive,
In this magic, we come alive.

Nighttime Revelries

When night descends and shadows play,
We revel in the end of day.
Stars awaken, bright against the dark,
Igniting joy, igniting spark.

With laughter ringing through the air,
We weave our dreams without a care.
The world glimmers in hues of grey,
As nighttime calls us out to play.

Beneath the blanket of the moon,
We sway and twirl to a joyful tune.
Lost in the magic of the night,
In every heart, a longing flight.

With each whispered secret shared,
In this moment, deeply ensnared.
Together we dance, till morning's morn,
In nighttime revelries, we are reborn.

Milton Keynes UK
Ingram Content Group UK Ltd.
UKHW021929011224
451790UK00005B/78